Rhyme Time 2

In this marvellous new collection by the compiler of *Rhyme Time*, there are around 200 poems on all the subjects close to the young child's heart – brothers and sisters, grans and grandpas, ghosts and witches, games, food, animals, nonsense. The poems have been selected for the vividness of the images they present, their rhythm and wordplay and their immediacy to young children.

Amongst the poets included are Shelley Silverstein, John Walsh, John Ciardi, Lilian Moore, Michael Rosen, Kit Wright, Colin West, Spike Milligan, Walter de la Mare and many more including Barbara Ireson herself. The book is a worthy follow-up to *Rhyme Time* which is now a classic anthology for children, and it will make an ideal introduction for young children and their parents to the joys of verse.

Barbara Ireson is the compiler of many sparkling poetry books for young children including *Rhyme Time, Over and Over Again* and *The Beaver Book of Funny Rhymes* on the Beaver list. A mother and young grandmother herself, she now lives and works in France.

Rhyme Time 2

Chosen by Barbara Ireson

Illustrated by Lesley Smith

Beaver Books

A Beaver Original

Published by Arrow Books Limited
62–65 Chandos Place, London WC2N 4NW

An imprint of Century Hutchinson Limited

London Melbourne Sydney Auckland
Johannesburg and agencies throughout
the world

First published 1984
Reprinted 1986

© Copyright this collection Barbara Ireson 1984
Illustrations © Century Hutchinson Ltd 1984

Set in Linoterm Bembo
by JH Graphics Limited, Reading

Printed and bound in Great Britain by
Cox & Wyman Ltd, Reading

ISBN 0 09 933810 6

Contents

Okay Everybody, Listen to This

Okay everybody, listen to this

Okay everybody, listen to this:
I am tired of being smaller
Than you
And them
And him
And trees and buildings.
So watch out
All you gorillas and adults
Beginning tomorrow morning
Boy
Am I going to be taller.

Karla Kuskin

Every few weeks someone looks at me

Every few weeks someone looks at me and says:
my you've grown
and then every few weeks someone says:
they've grown too long

and silver scissors come out of the drawer
and chip at my toes and run through my hair.

Now I don't like this one little bit.
I won't grow if I'm going to be chopped.
What's me is mine and I want to keep it
so either the scissors or my nails had better stop.

Michael Rosen

Hair

I despair
About hair
    With all the fuss
    For us
Of snipping
And clipping
    Of curling
    And twirling,
Of tying
And drying,
    And lopping
    And flopping,
And flurries
And worries,
    About strength,
    The length,
As it nears
The ears
    Or shoulder.
    When you're older
It turns grey
Or goes away
    Or leaves a fuzz
    Hair does!

Max Fatchen

I've had this shirt

I've had this shirt
that's covered in dirt
for years and years and years.

It used to be red
but I wore it in bed
and it went grey
'cos I wore it all day
for years and years and years.

The arms fell off
in the Monday wash
and you can see my vest
through the holes in the chest
for years and years and years.

As my shirt falls apart
I'll keep the bits
in a biscuit tin
on the mantelpiece
for years and years and years.

Michael Rosen

Hullabaloo!

Hullabaloo!
We'll race downstairs,
Splatter our porridge and bump the chairs,
And teach the budgie a thing or two!
Hullabalay baloo!

Hullabaloo!
We'll spend the day
In the most magnificent kind of way!
We'll shout whenever we want to shout,
And throw whatever we like about,
And turn the neighbourhood inside out!
Hullabaloo balay!

Hullabaloo!
The sun is high,
The clouds are shooshing across the sky,
Birds are soaring and winds are free,
Trees are tossing and we are WE!
(Nobody else we would rather be!)
Hullabalay baloo!

Hullabaloo!
The day is done.
We've had the funniest kind of fun,
And once for ever belied the fears
That morning laughter must end in tears,
. . . *We're* not crying! so sucks to you!
Hullabaloo . . . boohoo . . . boohoo!
Hullabaloo . . . boohoo!

Ursula Moray Williams

Tiptoe

Yesterday I skipped all day,
The day before I ran,
Today I'm going to tiptoe
Everywhere I can.
I'll tiptoe down the stairway.
I'll tiptoe through the door.
I'll tiptoe to the living room
And give an awful roar
And my father, who is reading,
Will jump up from his chair
And mumble something silly like
'I didn't see you there.'
I'll tiptoe to my mother
And give a little cough
And when she spins to see me
Why, I'll softly tiptoe off.
I'll tiptoe through the meadows,
Over hills and yellow sands
And when my toes get tired
Then I'll tiptoe on my hands.

Karla Kuskin

Every time I climb a tree

Every time I climb a tree
Every time I climb a tree
Every time I climb a tree
I scrape a leg
Or skin a knee
And every time I climb a tree
I find some ants
Or dodge a bee
And get the ants
All over me

And every time I climb a tree
Where have you been?
They say to me
But don't they know that I am free
Every time I climb a tree?
I like it best
To spot a nest
That has an egg
Or maybe three

And then I skin
The other leg
But every time I climb a tree
I see a lot of things to see
Swallows, rooftops and TV
And all the fields and farms there be
Every time I climb a tree
Though climbing may be good for ants
It isn't awfully good for pants
But still it's pretty good for me
Every time I climb a tree

David McCord

Eating an icicle, riding my bicycle

Eating an icicle, riding my bicycle,
Rolling along in the wind, rain and snow;
Chewing so happily, pedalling snappily
Backward and forward through gears high and low.
Icicle, bicycle, sometimes a tricycle,
Snappily, happily onward I go.

Anon

I found a silver dollar

I found a silver dollar,
But I had to pay the rent.
I found an alligator
But his steering-wheel was bent.
I found a little monkey,
So I took him to the zoo.
Then I found a sticky kiss and so
I brought it home to you.

Dennis Lee

Noise

I like noise.
The whoop of a boy, the thud of a hoof,
The rattle of rain on a galvanised roof,
The hub–bub of traffic, the roar of a train,
The throb of machinery numbing the brain,
The switching of wires in an overhead tram,
The rush of the wind, a door on the slam,
The boom of the thunder, the crash of the waves,
The din of a river that races and raves,
The crack of a rifle, the clank of a pail,
The strident tattoo of a swift slapping sail –
From any old sound that the silence destroys
Arises a gamut of soul–stirring joys.
I like noise.

J. Pope

Engineers

Pistons, valves and wheels and gears
That's the life of engineers
Thumping, chunking engines going
Hissing steam and whistles blowing.

There's not a place I'd rather be
Than working round machinery
Listening to that clanking sound
Watching all the wheels go round.

Jimmy Garthwaite

Do you or don't you

I like the tingling smell of tar,
And sticky ginger in a jar,
And drifting smoke from a cigar.
Do you?

I hate the stale damp smell of fogs
And matted hair of muddy dogs,
And slugs that lurk in stacked-up logs
Don't you?

I like the summer smell of sea,
And fishy smells about the quay
And strawberries and cream for tea.
Do you?

I hate the musty smell of mice,
And caged up birds, and uncooked rice,
And soft boiled eggs that aren't quite nice,
Don't you?

Anon

Mud

Mud is very nice to feel
All squishy-squash between the toes!
I'd rather wade in wiggly mud
Than smell a yellow rose.

Nobody else but the rosebush knows
How nice mud feels
Between the toes . . .

Polly Chase Boyden

My Dragon's Name is Jocelyn

Jocelyn, my dragon

My dragon's name is Jocelyn,
He's something of a joke.
For Jocelyn is very tame,
He doesn't like to maul or maim,
Or breathe a fearsome fiery flame;
He's much too smart to smoke.

And when I take him to the park
The children form a queue,
And say, 'What lovely eyes of red!'
As one by one they pat his head.
And Jocelyn is so well–bred,
He only eats a few!

Colin West

Under my bed

I've two large creatures under my bed
And no–one knows they're there.
I've fed them milk and fruit and bread
But did not stay to stare.

They've tails that lash
And teeth that gnash
And paws that thump
And heads that bump –

And I think I'll sleep in the shed.

Barbara Ireson

Advice to children

For a domestic, gentle pet,
A hippopotamus I'd get –
   They're very kind and mild.
I'm sure if you but purchase one
You'll find 'twill make a lot of fun
   For any little child.

Select one of a medium size,
With glossy fur and soft blue eyes,
   Then brush and comb him well.
With wreaths of flowers his forehead deck,
And from a ribbon round his neck
   Suspend a silver bell.

If it should be a rainy day,
Up in the nursery he will play
   With Baby, Tot and Ted;
Upon the rocking-horse he'll ride,
Or merrily he'll run and hide
   Beneath a chair or bed.

And when he wants to take a nap,
He'll cuddle up in Totty's lap,
   As quiet as a mouse.
Just try it, and you'll soon agree
A hippopotamus should be
   A pet in every house.

Carolyn Wells

Cottage

When I live in a Cottage
I shall keep in my Cottage

> Two different Dogs,
> Three creamy Cows,
> Four giddy Goats,
> Five pewter Pots,
> Six silver Spoons,
> Seven busy Beehives,
> Eight ancient Appletrees,
> Nine red Rosebushes,
> Ten teeming Teapots,
> Eleven chirping Chickens,
> Twelve cosy Cats with their kittenish
>   Kittens and
> One Blessed Baby in a Basket.

That's what I'll have when I live in my Cottage . . .

Eleanor Farjeon

Thin dog

I've got a dog as thin as a rail,
He's got fleas all over his tail;
Every time his tail goes flop,
The fleas on the bottom all hop to the top.

Anon

My dog

My dog is such a gentle soul,
    Although he's big it's true.
He brings the paper in his mouth.
    He brings the postman too.

Max Fatchen

Suzie's new dog

Your dog? What dog? You mean it? – that!
    I was about to leave a note
Pinned to a fish to warn my cat
    To watch for a mouse in an overcoat!

So that's a dog! Is it any breed
    That anyone ever knew – or guessed?
Oh, a Flea Terrier! Yes indeed.
    Well now, I *am* impressed!

I guess no robber will try your house
    Or even cut through your yard.
Not when he knows you have a mouse
    – I mean a dog – like that on guard!

You have to go? I'm glad you came!
    I don't see a thing like that
Just every day. Does it have a name?
    Fang, eh? Well, I must warn my cat.

John Ciardi

Poor John

I really think it would be better
If John the postman with his letter
Did not come to number four
And try to put it through the door.
A dog with teeth as big as knives
Waits there for him and then it dives
And sinks those teeth into his sack
And snarls and barks till John runs back.
The only thing that John can do
Is leave the post at number two.

Barbara Ireson

I'll buy a peacock bird

When I have a beard that's curly and weird,
I'll buy myself a peacock bird.
He'll shout, 'Hello, hello, hello,'
As on my lawns he'll to and fro.
Other birds will hop and glare
As he sheds feathers here and there.

I'll ask my Aunty Maud to tea
(For she has swans and a maple tree)
To view my peacock on my lawn
Who shouts 'Hello' from break of dawn,
And spy his mantle spreading wide
All shimmering blue and golden-eyed.

Modwena Sedgwick

I wish

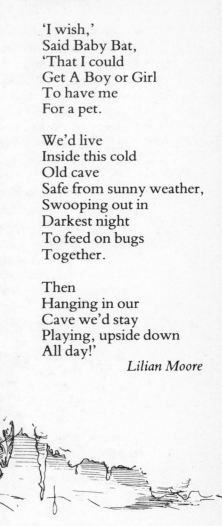

'I wish,'
Said Baby Bat,
'That I could
Get A Boy or Girl
To have me
For a pet.

We'd live
Inside this cold
Old cave
Safe from sunny weather,
Swooping out in
Darkest night
To feed on bugs
Together.

Then
Hanging in our
Cave we'd stay
Playing, upside down
All day!'

Lilian Moore

Cosy catnap

Pussy-kitten, pussy-cat,
purring on the kitchen mat,
How I like your furry tail
curl'd around you like a snail.

Pussy-kitten, pussy-cat,
purring on the kitchen mat;
fire tinkles in the grate,
clocks tick tip-toe, very late.

Pussy-kitten, pussy-cat,
purring on the kitchen mat;
hear the iron softly stamp
on steaming washing, warm and damp.

Pussy-kitten, pussy-cat,
purring on the kitchen mat,
squeeze your eyes right out of sight
and doze and blink and doze all night!

Pussy-kitten, pussy-cat,
purring on the kitchen mat;
purroo, purroo,
purroo, purroo,

Pussy-kitten, pussy-cat,
purrooing on the kitchen mat.

James Kirkup

Cat

The black cat yawns,
Opens her jaws,
Stretches her legs,
And shows her claws.

Then she gets up
And stands on four
Long stiff legs
And yawns some more.

She shows her sharp teeth,
She stretches her lip,
Her slice of tongue
Turns up at the tip.

Lifting herself
On her delicate toes,
She arches her back
As high as it goes.

She lets herself down
With particular care
And pads away
With her tail in the air.

Mary Britton Miller

Catnap

My cat sleeps
with her claws
clasped
and her long tail
curled.
My cat twitches
her tabby cheek
for the mice that
squeak
and the milk that
flows
by her pink, pink nose
in the purring warmth
of my cat's world.

Max Fatchen

Choosing their names

Our old cat has kittens three –
What do you think their names should be?

One is a tabby with emerald eyes,
    And a tail that's long and slender,
And into a temper she quickly flies
    If you ever by chance offend her,
        I think we shall call her this –
        I think we shall call her that –
Now, don't you think that Pepperpot
        Is a nice name for a cat?

One is black with a frill of white,
    And her feet are all white fur, too;
If you stroke her she carries her tail upright
    And quickly begins to purr, too!
        I think we shall call her this —
        I think we shall call her that —
Now, don't you think that Sootikin
        Is a nice name for a cat?

One is a tortoiseshell yellow and black,
    With plenty of white about him;
If you tease him, at once he sets up his back
    He's a quarrelsome one, ne'er doubt him.
        I think we shall call him this —
        I think we shall call him that —
Now, don't you think that Scratchaway
        Is a nice name for a cat?

Our old cat has kittens three
And I fancy these their names will be;
Pepperpot, Sootikin, Scratchaway — there!
Were ever kittens with these to compare?
And we call the old mother —
        Now, what do you think? —
    Tabitha Longclaws Tiddley Wink.

                            Thomas Hood

A kitten

He's nothing much but fur
And two round eyes of blue,
He has a giant purr
And a midget mew.

He darts and pats the air,
He starts and pricks his ear,
When there is nothing there
For him to see and hear.

He runs around in rings,
But why we cannot tell;
With sideways leaps he springs
At things invisible –

Then half-way through a leap
His started eyeballs close,
And he drops off to sleep
With one paw on his nose.

Eleanor Farjeon

Billy Booster

Billy Billy Booster
Had a little rooster,
The rooster died
And Billy cried.
Poor Billy Booster.

Anon

Missing

Has anybody seen my mouse?

I opened his box for half a minute,
Just to make sure he was really in it,
And while I was looking, he jumped outside!
I tried to catch him, I tried, I tried . . .
I think he's somewhere about the house.
Has *anyone* seen my mouse?

Uncle John, have you seen my mouse?

Just a small sort of mouse, a dear little brown one,
He came from the country, he wasn't a town one,
So he'll feel all lonely in a London Street;
Why, what could he possibly find to eat?

He must be somewhere, I'll ask Aunt Rose:
Have you seen a mouse with a woffelly nose?
Oh, somewhere about –
He's just got out . . .

Hasn't *anybody* seen my mouse?

A. A. Milne

Lost and found

LOST:
A Wizard's loving pet
Rather longish.
Somewhat scaly.
May be hungry or
upset.
Please feed daily.

P.S. Reward

FOUND:
A dragon
breathing fire.
Flails his scaly
tail
in ire.
Would eat twenty LARGE meals
daily
if we let him
Please
Come and get him.

P.S. No reward necessary.

Lilian Moore

Goldfish

One small Fish in a
Polythene bag;
Can't swim round, can
Only look sad.
Take a pair of scissors,
Snip a quick hole:
Down flops water
And Fish into a bowl!

She waits a little moment,
Flips her tail free,
Then off into circles
As frisk as can be.
Dash-about – splash-about –
Do what you wish:
You're mine, you black-spotted
Cheeky-eyed
Fish!

John Walsh

Wanted

Has anyone got
A puppy to spare,
A cat or a rabbit
Or even a hare?

I'd cherish a pony,
I'd care for a horse,
If I'm offered a camel,
I'd love it, of course.

I'd take in a hamster,
I'd quite like a rat,
A toad would be welcome,
Or even a bat.

A beetle that's friendly
Would find that I'm kind,
Snake, lizard or earthworm,
I'm sure I don't mind.

I don't mind how big,
I don't mind how small,
I just want a pet
That can walk, fly or crawl.

Barbara Ireson

The Wiggley-Woggley Men

The Wiggley-Woggley men

Oh the Wiggley-Woggley men
They don't get up till ten
They run about
Then give a shout
And back to bed again!

Spike Milligan

Names

Murgatroyd Stephen Montgomery James.
Did you ever hear such a collection of names?
Murgatroyd after his father, you see.
Stephen because of his uncle, that's me.
His mother chose Monty, and she was emphatic;
While James, said his aunties, was aristocratic
So he was christened, but isn't it silly?
The only name anyone calls him is Billy.

Norman Hunter

Huffer and Cuffer

Huffer, a giant ungainly and gruff
encountered a giant called Cuffer.
said Cuffer to Huffer, I'M ROUGH AND I'M TOUGH,
said Huffer to Cuffer, I'M TOUGHER.

they shouted such insults as BOOB and BUFFOON
and OVERBLOWN BLOWHARD and BLIMP
and BLUSTERING BLUBBER and BLOATED
    BALLOON
and SHATTERBRAIN, SHORTY and SHRIMP.

then Huffer and Cuffer exchanged mighty blows,
they basted and battered and belted,
they chopped to the neck and they bopped in the nose
and they pounded and pummeled and pelted.

they pinched and they punched and they smacked
    and they whacked
and they rocked and they socked and they smashed.
and they rapped and they slapped and they
    throttled and thwacked
and they thumped and they bumped and they bashed.

they cudgeled each other on top of the head
with swipes of the awfulest sort.
and now they are no longer giants, instead
they both are exceedingly short.

Jack Prelutsky

Juniper Jim

Juniper Jim
Is very thin
As well as very old,
And if it wasn't for
The length of his beard
He would catch his death of cold.

John Jenkins

Mrs Golightly

Mrs Golightly's goloshes
   Are roomy and large;
Through water she slithers and sloshes,
   As safe as a barge.

When others at home must be stopping,
   To market she goes,
And returns later on with her shopping
   Tucked into her toes.

James Reeves

Be quiet

The world's greatest snorer
   Was Barrington Brown.
His snores shook the windows
   And rattled the town.

The people grew frantic
   And fearful with fright,
And cried to each other,
   'What happens tonight?'

They lullabyed softly
   But who could ignore
The deafening noise
   Of that terrible snore?

They tied up their heads
   And their eardrums they bound,
But nothing could soften
   That thundering sound.

They made a giant clothes-peg
   And placed on his nose.
With one mighty snore
   Like a rocket it rose.

So they all left the town
   In their cars and their carts,
'We must be away
   Before Barrington starts.'

Then Barrington woke,
   'Where's everyone gone?'
And then he turned over
   And went snoring on!

Max Fatchen

Pete, Pete

Pete, Pete, is always neat
From the top of his head to the soles of his feet;
He hasn't got any hair at all,
So he buffs his bonce like a billiard ball.

Anon

The sitter

Mrs McTwitter the baby-sitter,
I think she's a little bit crazy.
She thinks a baby-sitter's suppose
To sit upon the baby.

Shel Silverstei

The old maiden from Fife

There was an old maiden from Fife,
Who had never been kissed in her life;
Along came a cat,
And she said, 'I'll kiss that!'
But the cat answered, 'Not on your life!'

Anon

Fred

There was a pop singer called Fred
Who sang through the top of his head.
    It came as a blow
    When the notes were too low
So he sang through his toenails instead.

Max Fatchen

Hickenthrift and Hickenloop

Hickenthrift and Hickenloop
    Stood fourteen mountains high:
They'd wade the wind, they'd have to stoop
    To let the full moon by.

Their favourite sport, played on a court,
    Was called Kick Down the Castle:
They'd stamp their boots, those vast galoots,
    Till king lay low as vassal.

One day while spooning hot rock soup
    From a volcano crater,
Said Hickenthrift, 'Hey, Hickenloop,
    Who of us two is greater?'

Across the other's jagged brow
    Dark thunder seemed to drift,
And Hickenloop, with one swift swoop,
    Ate straight through Hickenthrift.

X. J. Kennedy

Lazy Lucy

Lazy Lucy
lay in bed.
Lazy Lucy's
mother said:
'You will drive
your mother crazy.
Upsy–daisy,
Lucy Lazy!'
To her mom
said Lazy Lucy,
'Little children
can't be choosy
(though I would
prefer to snooze
in my bed
if I could choose).
I will not
drive Mamma crazy,
I will not
at all be lazy,
I will jump
right out of bed
– and be Sleepy Lu
instead.'

N. M. Bodecker

I Like it When it's Mizzly

I like it when it's mizzly

I like it when it's mizzly
and just a little drizzly
so everything looks far away
and make–believe and frizzly.

I like it when it's foggy
and sounding very froggy.
I even like it when it rains
on streets and weepy windowpanes
and catkins in the poplar tree
and *me*.

Aileen Fisher

The dark gray clouds

The dark gray clouds,
the great gray clouds,
the black rolling clouds are elephants
going down to the sea for water.
They draw up the water in their trunks.
They march back again across the sky.
They spray the earth again with the water,
and men say it is raining.

Natalia M. Belting

Windscreen wipers

I sit in our car and to and fro,
In front of my nose, the wipers go.
To and fro, to and fro,
And wipe away the rain and snow.

Barbara Ireson

Thunder and lightning

About wind and rain,
I never complain,
But I wonder why thunder
And lightning's so frightening?

Barbara Ireson

Summer song

By the sand between my toes,
By the waves behind my ears,
By the sunburn on my nose,
By the little salty tears
That make rainbows in the sun
When I squeeze my eyes and run,
By the way the seagulls screech,
Guess where I am? *At the* . . .!
By the way the children shout
Guess what happened? *School is* . . .!
By the way I sing this song
Guess if summer lasts too long:
You must answer Right or . . .!

John Ciardi

Seasons

Spring is showery, flowery, bowery,
Summer: hoppy, croppy, poppy;
Autumn: wheezy, sneezy, freezy;
Winter: slippy, drippy, nippy.

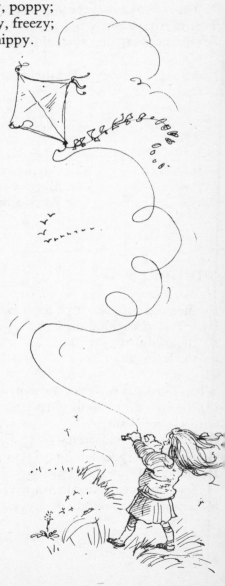

To a red kite

Fling
yourself
upon the sky.

Take the string
you need.
Ride high

high
above the park.
Tug and buck
and lark
with the wind.

Touch a cloud,
red kite.
Follow the wild geese
in their flight.

Lilian Moore

Granny

Through every nook and every cranny
The wind blew in on poor old Granny,
Around her knees, into each ear
(And up her nose as well, I fear).

All through the night the wind grew worse,
It nearly made the vicar curse.
The top had fallen off the steeple
Just missing him (and other people).

It blew on man; it blew on beast.
It blew on nun; it blew on priest.
It blew the wig off Auntie Fanny –
But most of all, it blew on Granny.

Spike Milligan

The Britons of old

The Britons of old had a mode,
Of wearing smart costumes of woad –
   A kind of blue paint –
   They must have looked quaint,
I bet they looked cold when it snowed!

Langford Reed

Snowman

'Twas the first day of the springtime,
And the snowman stood alone
As the winter snows were melting,
And the pine trees seemed to groan,
'Ah, you poor sad smiling snowman,
You'll be melting by and by.'
Said the snowman, 'What a pity,
For I'd like to see July.
Yes, I'd like to see July, and please don't ask me why.
But I'd like to, yes I'd like to, oh I'd like to see July.'

Chirped a robin, just arriving,
'Seasons come and seasons go,
And the greatest ice must crumble
When it's flowers' time to grow.
And as one thing is beginning
So another thing must die,
And there's never been a snowman
Who has ever seen July.
No, they never see July, no matter how they try.
No, they never ever, never ever, never see July.'

But the snowman sniffed his carrot nose
And said, 'At least I'll try.'
And he bravely smiled his frosty smile
And blinked his coal-black eye.
And there he stood and faced the sun
A blazin' from the sky –
And I really cannot tell you
If he ever saw July.
Did he ever see July? You can guess as well as I
If he ever, if he never, if he ever saw July.

Shel Silverstein

Questions! Questions! Questions!

What do you know? It's going to snow.
How can you tell? By sniff and by smell.
What do you sniff? The wind off the cliff.
What do you smell? The ice in the well.
What do they say? It's coming this way.
How deep will it be? Two fathoms or three.
What shall I do? Stay here till it's through.
What shall I eat? Ox tail and pig's feet.
Where shall I sleep? In the pen with the sheep.
What if it gets colder? Put a lamb on your shoulder.
What if it melts? You can go somewhere else.
Then what will I get? Your feet good and wet.
How will I dry them? Bring them here and I'll fry them.
What of my dad? He'll say they taste bad.
What of my mother? She'll cuddle your brother.
What about you? I'll be glad when you're through.

John Ciardi

Footsteps

Our lawn, which yesterday was green,
Today is nowhere to be seen.
The snow fell heavily all night
Leaving a covering of white.
It's smooth as icing and as clean.
Nothing has spoiled it. No one's been.
But in a minute I shall go
In wellingtons across the snow
And every footstep that I take
Will spoil the icing on the cake

Barbara Ireson

Snowy morning

Wake
Gently this morning
to a different day.
Listen.

There is no bray
of buses,
no brake growls,
no siren howls and
no horns
blow.

There is only
the silence
of a city
hushed
by snow.

Lilian Moore

Shrieks at Midnight

Shrieks at midnight

I do like ogres –
There's something about them
So utterly ruthless
And yet absurd!
    I don't believe in them.
Yet I shiver
The very instant
I hear the word –
FE-FI-FO-FUM!

Dorothy Brown Thompson

Grim

Beside the blaze of forty fires
        Giant Grim doth sit,
Roasting a thick-wooled mountain sheep
        Upon an iron spit.
Above him wheels the winter sky,
        Beneath him, fathoms deep,
Lies hidden in the valley mists
        A village fast asleep –
Save for one restive hungry dog
        That, snuffing towards the height,
Smells Grim's broiled supper-meat, and spie
        His watch-fire twinkling bright.

Walter de la Mare

The Troll Bridge

This is the Bridge
of the
Terrible Troll.
No one goes
by
without paying
a toll,
a terrible toll
to the Troll.

It's no place to
loll, to
linger or
stroll,
to sing or to
play.

So if ever you
ride
to the
opposite side,
be ready to
pay
the terrible troll
I mean terrible toll
to the Terrible Toll –
I mean Troll.

Lilian Moore

A giant named Stanley

I ain't one to complain,
Don't get me wrong;
Something's been buggin' me
For far too long.
My mother's an angel,
My father – a saint!
And in all of these years,
I've but one complaint.
I love my mother,
My father I prize;
But why did they give
A kid of my size
  The gentle name of Stanley?
In the fabled days of yore,
Our tribe was famed for blood and gore:
  Cormoran and Blunderbore,
  Blunderbeard and Thunderoar,
  Gog, Magog, Asundertore!
  But not a single Stanley.
I'd have taken Blunderbore,
Shuttlecock or Battledore,
Close-your-mouth or Shut-the-door!
  Anything but Stanley!
  Oh, anything but Stanley!

Michael Patrick Hearn

Fear

From time to time I have to go
Close by a haunted house I know.
I never look behind for fear
Someone or something may appear.

Sometimes I have to take a street
Which echoes with my running feet,
I never look behind for fear
Someone or something may appear.

And if I have to cross the park
At midnight when it's very dark,
I never look behind for fear
Someone or something may appear.

A hooting owl gives me a fright
If I go home alone at night.
I never look behind for fear
Someone or something may appear.

I hurry under ancient trees
Where creatures rustle through the leaves.
I never look behind for fear
Someone or something may appear.

But next year I'll be eight and then
I'll go out in the dark and when
I'm all alone you'll hear me shout,
'I'm not afraid, so please come out!'

Barbara Ireson

Night sounds

Midnight's bell goes ting, ting, ting, ting, ting,
Then dogs do howl, and not a bird does sing
But the nightingale, and she cries twit, twit, twit;
Owls then on every bough do sit;
Ravens croak on chimneys' tops;
The cricket in the chamber hops;
The nibbling mouse is not asleep,
But he goes peep, peep, peep, peep, peep;
    And the cats cry mew, mew, mew,
    And still the cats cry mew, mew, mew.

Thomas Middleton

Running home

I look behind. Is someone there?
It's difficult to see.
The street is dark, I race along
And footsteps follow me.

Who's coming round the corner?
Who kicked that rolling can?
Who's hiding there behind the gate?
Who crouched behind that van?

The footsteps stop. I scan the street.
Someone's behind a tree.
Long shadows stretch across the ground.
Who's coming after me?

Barbara Ireson

The dog

I lie in bed and through the dark
I hear a dog begin to bark,
A sharp and urgent, fearsome sound
That fills the countryside around.
He's telling someone to beware.
What is it that he knows is there?

Barbara Ireson

Teeny tiny ghost

A teeny tiny ghost
no bigger than a mouse
at most,
lived in a great big house.

It's hard to haunt
a great big house
when you're a teeny tiny ghost
no bigger than a mouse,
at most.

He did what he could do.

So every dark and stormy night –
the kind that shakes a house with fright –
if you stood still and listened right,
you'd hear a
teeny
tiny
BOO!

Lilian Moore

Whose boo is whose?

Two ghosts I know once traded heads
And shrieked and shook their sheets to shreds –
'You're me!' yelled one, 'and me, I'm you!
Now who can boo the loudest boo?'

'Me!' cried the other, and for proof
He booed a boo that scared the roof
Right off our house. The TV set
Jumped higher than a jumbo jet.

The first ghost snickered. 'Why, you creep,
Call that a boo? That feeble beep?
Hear *this*!' – and sucking in a blast
Of wind, he puffed his sheet so vast

And booed so hard, a passing goose
Lost all its down. The moon shook loose
And fell and smashed to smithereens –
Stars scattered like spilled jellybeans.

'How's that for booing, boy? I win,'
Said one. The other scratched a chin
Where only bone was – 'Win or lose?
How can we tell whose boo is whose?'

X. J. Kennedy

Singing ghost

At the circus I was watching
Two dogs and a parakeet
When a ghost appeared before me
Dancing without any feet.
'Hey,' I said, 'what are you doing?'
He said, 'Giving you a treat.'
'Look,' I said, 'I'm at the circus.
Don't you know you can't compete?'
He said, 'No, my act's the greatest,'
And he burst into a song:
Oola oola woo balloola
Oola woola woola bong.
'Stop,' I said, 'I'll get in trouble,
You are being such a pest.'
In a moment cops appeared and
Threatened me with quick arrest.
'Come along with us,' they ordered,
'Songs that interrupt won't do.'
So they took me off to prison
And the singing ghost came too.

Steven Kroll

Who's scared now?

I'm warning you.
Don't scare me.
Don't go 'Boo'.
Will you?
Don't say you're from space
Or some awful place.
That you're a deep–sea creature
Or a late–night movie monster,
Will you?
Because –
ZAP!
POW!
I'm disintegrating you now.
Click,
Tick!
You are reassembled
And changed,
Your matter
Rearranged,
Thirteen million light years away,
If it's a day,
On the planet Zen,
With a scratchy pen,
Doing four million lines,
In the Homework Mines.
And it serves you right
For frightening me last night.

Max Fatchen

Sir Hector

Sir Hector was a spectre
And he loved a lady ghost;
At midnight he'd collect her
And he'd drive her to the coast.

And there upon the shingle
They would rattle all their bones,
And ocean sounds would mingle
With their melancholy moans.

Colin West

Fairy story

I went into the wood one day
And there I walked and lost my way

When it was so dark I could not see
A little creature came to me

He said if I would sing a song
The time would not be very long

But first I must let him hold my hand tight
Or else the wood would give me a fright

I sang a song, he let me go
But now I am home again there is nobod

The games of night

When the ghost comes, I don't see her
I smell the licorice drops in her pocket.
I climb out of bed, I draw her bath.
She has come a long way, and I know she's tired.

By the light of the moon, the water splashes.
By the light of the stars, the soap leaps,
it dives, it pummels the air,
it scrubs off the dust of not-seeing.

and I see her sandals, black like mine,
and I see her dress, white like mine.
Little by little, she comes clear
She rises up in a skin of water

As long as the water shines, I can see her.
As long as I see her, we can play
by the light of the moon on my bed,
by the light of the stars on my bear
till the sun opens its eye, the sun that wakes things,
the sun that doesn't believe in ghosts . . .

Nancy Willard

The small ghostie

When it's late and it's dark
And everyone sleeps . . . shhh shhh shhh,
Into our kitchen
A small ghostie creeps . . . shhh shhh shhh.

We hear knockings and raps
And then rattles and taps,

Then he clatters and clangs
And he batters and bangs,

And he whistles and yowls
And he screeches and howls . . .

So we pull up our covers over our heads
And we block up our ears and WE STAY IN OUR BEDS.

Barbara Ireson

I never saw

I never saw
            a ghost on stilts
a witch wrapped up
            in patchwork quilts
a dragon
in a wagon
or a wizard wearing kilts.

I said
I never *did*.
I didn't say
I never *may*.

Lilian Moore

Fingummy . . .

Fingummy's fat
And Fingummy's small,
And Fingummy lives
With the boots in the hall.

If Fingummy bites,
If Fingummy tears,
If Fingummy chases you
Up the stairs
Shout 'Bumble-Bee Soup
And Bluebottle Jam',
And run up to bed as fast as you can!

'Cos Fingummy lives
Where there's never no light
And Fingummy makes
The dark sounds of the night,
And Fingummy's fat
And Fingummy's small
And Fingummy lives
In the dark, in the hall . . .   *Mike Harding*

What night would it be?

If the moon shines
On the black pines
And an owl flies
And a ghost cries
And the hairs rise
On the back
    on the back
        on the back of your neck –

If you look quick
At the moon-slick
On the black air
And what goes there
Rides a broom-stick
And if things pick
At the back
   at the back
      at the back of your neck –

Would you know then
By the small men
With the lit grins
And with no chins,
By the owl's *hoo*,
And the ghost's *boo*,
By the Tom Cat,
And the Black Bat
On the night air,
And the thing there,
By the thing,
   by the thing,
      by the dark thing there

(Yes, you do,
   yes, you do
      know the thing I mean)

That it's now,
   that it's now,
      that it's – Halloween!

John Ciardi

The witches' ride

Over the hills
Where the edge of the light
Deepens and darkens
To ebony night,
Narrow hats high
Above yellow bead eyes,
The tatter-haired witches
Ride through the skies.
Over the seas
Where the flat fishes sleep
Wrapped in the slap of the slippery deep,
Over the peaks
Where the black trees are bare,
Where boney birds quiver
They glide through the air.
Silently humming
A horrible tune,
They sweep through the stillness
To sit on the moon.

Karla Kuskin

Hallowe'en

Tonight is the night
When dead leaves fly
Like witches on switches
Across the sky,
When elf and sprite
Flit through the night
On a moony sheen.

Tonight is the night
When leaves make a sound
Like a gnome in his home
Under the ground,
When spooks and trolls
Creep out of holes
Mossy and green.

Tonight is the night
When pumpkins stare
Through sheaves and leaves
Everywhere,
When ghoul and ghost
And goblin host
Dance round their queen.
It's Hallowe'en!

Harry Behn

The witch's song

Hey! Cackle! Hey!
Let's have fun today.

All shoelaces will have knots.
No knots will untie.
Every glass of milk will spill.
Nothing wet will dry.
Every pencil point will break.
And everywhere in town
Peanut–buttered bread will drop
Upside down.

Hey! Hey! Hey!
Have a pleasant day.

Lilian Moore

Fat old witch

The strangest sight
I've ever seen
Was a fat old witch
In a flying machine.

The witch flew high,
The witch flew low,
The witch flew fast,
The witch flew slow,
The witch flew up,
The witch flew down,
She circled all
Around the town.
Then, turning left
And turning right,
She disappeared
Into the night.

That fat old witch
In a flying machine
Is the strangest sight
I've ever seen.
Of course it happened
On Hallowe'en.

Leland B. Jacobs

Bedtime story

'Tell me a story,'
Says Witch's Child,

'About the Beast
So fierce and wild.

About a Ghost
That shrieks and groans,

A Skeleton
That rattles bones,

About a Monster
Crawly–creepy.

Something nice
To make me sleepy.'

Lilian Moore

The witch's garden

In the witch's
garden
the gate is open
wide.

'Come inside,'
says the
witch.
'Dears,
come inside.

No flowers
in *my* garden,
nothing mint-y
nothing chive-y

Come inside,
come inside.
See my lovely
poison ivy.'

Lilian Moore

Frogday

I met a witch on Wednesday,
And Crabtree was her name;
I saw her next on Friday
And called her that again.
'Look here,' she said – her voice was bleak –
'We witches often change.
On Tuesdays I'm called Fenugreek,
On Thursdays simply Mange
And if on Mondays you should call,
You'll find my name is Lizard:
On Sundays I've no name at all,
On Saturdays I'm Wizard.
But Friday is a witch's own,
The witchiest day of all –
I'm Magpie and I'm Megaphone,
I'm Grimsdyke and I'm Gall;
And when I'm feeling really bad
I'm Bogey, Boot and Blog.
Now if you forget all that, my lad –
You'll turn into a frog!'

Shelagh McGee

Always Sprinkle Pepper in your Hair

Always sprinkle pepper

Always sprinkle pepper in your hair,
Always sprinkle pepper in your hair.
For then if you are kidnapped by a Wild Barbazzoop,
Who sells you to a Ragged Hag
Who wants you for her soup,
She'll pick you up and sniff you,
And then she'll sneeze 'Achooo,'
And say, 'My tot, you're much too hot,
I fear you'll never do.'
And with a shout she'll throw you out,
And you'll run away from there,
And soon you will be safe at home a–sittin' in your chair,
If you always, always, always,
Always, always, always, always,
Always, always, always, sprinkle pepper in your hair.

Shel Silverste

Triolet

I wish I were a jelly fish
That cannot fall downstairs:
Of all the things I wish to wish
I wish I were a jelly fish
That hasn't any cares,
And doesn't even have to wish
'I wish I were a jelly fish
That cannot fall downstairs.'

G. K. Chesterton

Shopping list

I'm going on a shopping trip
For items that I'm short of.
Like lizards' legs and goose grease
And some other things I've thought of:
It's best to get them straightaway
Before the price goes up –
I must remember dragon's blood,
And oil of buttercup.
I'll need some wind for gas-bags.
Some wart–cream for my toad –
I'm out of stock of cochineal,
Perhaps I could use woad.
I want some jolly robins
To make a feather-brain:
I'd better wear my mackintosh.
My bunions forecast rain.
I'm going in a minute.
Just let me find a broom –
There's such a lot to carry –
Well, that cat won't have much room!

Shelagh McGee

Kangaroo – kangaroo!

The kangaroo of Australia
Lives on the burning plain,
He keeps on leaping in the air
'Cos it's hot when he lands again.

Spike Milligan

Oh, such silliness!

Oh, such silliness!
Silly willy-nilliness,
Dopey hillybilliness,
Rolling down the hilliness!

Oh, such craziness!
First of April Dayziness,
Giddy, goopy gayziness,
Bumpy dumb horseplayziness!

Oh, such sappiness!
Ridiculous slaphappiness,
Throw away his cappiness,
Jump into his lappiness!

Oh, such hilarity!
Falling down the stairity,
Tipping over chairity,
Shaving off your hairity!

Ghostliness and ghoulishness!
Push him in the poolishness,
Staying home from schoolishness –
Oh, such foolishness!

William Cole

Kangaroo shoe

A kangaroo
From Woolloomooloo
Found himself
A worn–out shoe.
He's getting tired
Hopping around
With one foot only
On the ground.
So if you see
This kangaroo
Please try to find
Another shoe.

Dorothy Barnham

Do you know the man?

Do you know the man with the flowers growing
Out of the top of his head?
Yellow flowers,
Purple flowers,
Orange, green, and red.
Growing there
Just like hair
Out of the top of his head.
(Yes, you heard just what I said –
Out of the top of his head.)

Shel Silverstein

'Quack!' said the billy-goat

'Quack!' said the billy-goat,
'Oink!' said the hen.
'Miaow!' said the little chick
Running in the pen.

'Hobble-gobble!' said the dog.
'Cluck!' said the sow.
'Tu-whit tu-whoo!' the donkey said.
'Baa!' said the cow.

'Hee-haw!' the turkey cried.
The duck began to moo.
And all at once the sheep went
'Cock-a-doodle-doo!'

The owl coughed and cleared his throat
And he began to bleat.
'Bow-wow!' said the cock
Swimming in the leat.

'Cheep-cheep!' said the cat
As she began to fly.
'Farmer's been and laid an egg –
That's the reason why.'

Charles Causley

Granny's boot

Granny in her bed one night
Heard a little squeak!
And then a little
Peck-peck-peck
Like something with a beak
Then something that went Binkle-Bonk
Ickle-tickle-toot
And all of it was coming
From inside Grandma's boot!
Then the boot began to *hop*
It went into the hall
And then from deep inside the boot
Came a Tarzan call
The sound of roaring lions
The screech of a cockatoo
Today that boot is in a cage
Locked in the London Zoo.

Spike Milligan

The longest tale about the longest tail

I am the longest, the longest, the strongest,
Yes, I am the longestest worm in the world.
I am so long, so far I extend,
That I haven't ever no never not ever
Oh, I've never ever seen my other end.

Well, I have been thinking and thinking and blinking
Yes, I have been thinking one very fine day
That I should flip, take a long trip
Until I meet it, oh meet it and greet it
Yes, until I meet with my opposite tip.

So there I was crawling and crawling and rolling
Yes, there I was crawling that very fine day
When suddenly there, just around the bend
I saw it, I know it, I know that I saw it
I saw it, I know it was my other end!

I was so happy, so happy and peppy
Yes, I was so terribly happy and glad
That I cried: 'Hail, you must be my tail!'
And then it wiggled and wriggled and giggled
And then it suddenly spoke up and said:

'I am the longest, the longest, the strongest,
Yes, I am the longestest worm in the world . . .'

Alexander Resnikoff

Multikertwigo

I saw the Multikertwigo
Standing on his head,
He was looking at me sideways
And this is what he said:
'Sniddle Iddle Ickle Thwack
Nicki–Nacki–Noo
Biddle–diddle Dicky–Dack
Tickle-tockle-too!'
None of this made sense to me,
Maybe it does to you.

Spike Milligan

Bad and good

Do you know what is bad?
I'll tell you what is bad:
To sprinkle catchup on your dad,
'Specially when he's mad.

Do you know what is good?
I'll tell you what is good:
To keep your foot out of your food
When mommy says you should.

Alexander Resnikoff

Bear in there

There's a Polar Bear
In our Frigidaire —
He likes it 'cause it's cold in there.
With his seat in the meat
And his face in the fish
And his big hairy paws
In the buttery dish,
He's nibbling the noodles,
He's munching the rice,
He's slurping the soda,
He's licking the ice.
And he lets out a roar
If you open the door.
And it gives me a scare
To know he's in there —
That Polary Bear
In our Fridgitydaire.

Shel Silverstein

The Ogglewop

The Ogglewop is tall and wide,
And though he looks quite passive,
He's crammed with boys and girls inside,
— That's why he is so massive!

Colin West

Mr 'Gator

Elevator operator
P. Cornelius Alligator,
when his passengers
were many,
never
ever
passed up
any:
when his passengers
were few
always managed
to make do.
When they told him:
'Mister 'Gator!
quickly
in your elevator
take us
to the nineteenth floor!'
they were never
seen no more.

N. M. Bodecker

Don't ever seize a weasel by the tail

You should never squeeze a weasel
for you might displease the weasel,
and don't ever seize a weasel by the tail.

Let his tail blow in the breeze
if you pull it, he will sneeze
for the weasel's constitution tends to be a little frail.

Yes, the weasel wheezes easily,
the weasel freezes easily,
the weasel's tan complexion rather suddenly turns pale.

So don't displease or tease a weasel,
squeeze or freeze or wheeze a weasel,
and don't ever seize a weasel by the tail, by the tail.

Jack Prelutsky

My Obnoxious Brother Bobby

My obnoxious brother Bobby

My obnoxious brother Bobby
Has a most revolting hobby;
There behind the garden wall is
Where he captures creepy–crawlies.

Grannies, aunts and baby cousins
Come to our house in their dozens,
But they disappear discreetly
When they see him smiling sweetly.

For they know, as he approaches,
In his pockets are cockroaches,
Spiders, centipedes and suchlike;
All of which they do not much like.

As they head towards the lobby,
Bidding fond farewells to Bobby,
How they wish he'd change his habits
And keep guinea pigs or rabbits.

But their wishes are quite futile,
For he thinks that bugs are cute. I'll
Finish now, but just remind you:
Bobby could be right behind you!

Colin West

It isn't

It isn't a bud
that turns into a rose,
but it grows.

It isn't a set
of musical bells,
but it yells.

It isn't a hippo
with triple chins,
but it grins.

It isn't a goat
eating paper bags,
but it na–aa–ags.

It isn't a vine
wrapped 'round a tree,
but it trails after me.

It's no other
than
my baby brother.

Eve Merriam

83

Brother

Why must we have him,
This new little brother?
He bawls all the time
And is really a bother.

He's not quiet like Teddy,
He does nothing but cry,
They say I must love him,
But I don't think I'll try.

He hasn't much hair
He's all wrinkled and red.
I'd much rather have
A new spaceman instead.

Yes, you may have him.
Please take him away . . .
But perhaps we should keep him
For just one more day.

Look how he laughs
When I stroke his small head.
I think that he knows
That it's me by his bed.

And, perhaps he would miss me,
I am his big brother.
There's just him and me
And our Daddy and Mother.

Barbara Ireson

Grandpa dropped his glasses

Grandpa dropped his glasses once
In a pot of dye,
And when he put them on again
He saw a purple sky.
Purple birds were rising up
From a purple hill,
Men were grinding purple cider
At a purple mill.
Purple Adeline was playing
With a purple doll,
Little purple dragon flies
Were crawling up the wall.
And at the supper-table
He got crazy as a loon
From eating purple apple dumplings
With a purple spoon.

Leroy F. Jackson

Babbling and gabbling

My Granny's an absolute corker,
My Granny's an absolute cracker,
But she's Britain's speediest talker
And champion yackety-yacker!

Everyone's fond of my Granny,
Everyone thinks she's nice,
But before you can say Jack Robinson,
My Granny's said it twice!

Kit Wright

My Granny is a witch

I'm a very small boy
and my Granny is a witch
I love my Granny very much
but she's a witch.
Once on a summer night
she got up and went into the kitchen
I crept after her
and there was a strong smell of onions
up hopped Granny on to the frying-pan
and burst out singing ever so loud
and I was ever so frightened
she beckoned to me
and together we flew out of the window
I held on as hard as I could
because the earth below was like a cup
peacocks were strutting over it
and swans swam all in white
it glittered like a Christmas tree
and we dropped into a cake shop
Granny stole some tarts
and I ate them
and Granny ate even more
because she was very tired
and then we came back on a pony
we got undressed ever so quietly
and slipped into bed
Granny told me not to make a noise.
Granny's very kind
it's a pity she's a witch though.

Arkady Mikhailov

Poor Gran

On this subject I'm sorry to speak
It happened on Saturday week.
> They loaded poor Gran
> In a furniture van
And auctioned her off as antique.

Max Fatchen

Jo

You say that Jo has made you late,
You say that Jo has dropped a plate.
You say he never leaves your side,
But when I'm here he seems to hide.
Sometimes I think he must be shy,
Or is it that he's very sly?
He breaks your toys, he picks my flowers,
He keeps you out for hours and hours.
Poor secret Jo, it seems a shame
He always has to take the blame.
I wonder is it really true
It's always him and never you?

Barbara Ireson

Did you?

Having little kids around, they say, is truly bliss;
But did you ever hear of any little kid like this?

He swallows pits,
Has temper fits,
Spills the ink,
And clogs the sink.
And, oh my gosh!
He hates to wash!
He plays with matches,
And grabs and snatches.
He scrawls on walls,
And sprawls and bawls,
And argues and fights,
And kicks and bites . . .
You say you never heard of
    any kid like that, you do —
Well, I know one who's
    just like that and it's
                        Y
                          O
                            U!

William Cole

Cousin Jane

Yesterday my cousin Jane
Said she was an aeroplane,
But I wanted further proof —
So I pushed her off the roof.

Colin West

Music makers

My Auntie plays the piccolo
My uncle plays the flute,
They practise every night at ten
Tweetly tweet *Toot-toot*!

My Granny plays the banjo,
My Grandad plays the drum,
They practise every night at nine
Plankety plank *Bumm-bumm*!!

My sister plays the tuba
My brother plays guitar,
They practise every night at six
Twankity *Oom-pa-pa*!!!

My mother plays the mouth organ,
My daddy plays oboe,
They practise every night at eight
Pompity-pom suck–blow!!!!

Anon

Billy Batter

Billy Batter,
What's the matter?
How come you're so sad?
 I lost my cat
 In the laundromat,
And a dragon ran off with my dad,
 My dad—
A dragon ran off with my dad!

Billy Batter,
What's the matter?
How come you're so glum?
 I ripped my jeans
 On the Coke machine,
And a monster ran off with my mum,
 My mum—
A monster ran off with my mum!

Billy Batter,
Now you're better—
Happy as a tack!
 The dragon's gone
 To Saskatchewan;
 The monster fell
 In a wishing-well;
 The cat showed up
 With a new-born pup;
 I fixed the rips
 With potato chips,
And my dad and my mum came back,
 Came back—
My dad and my mum came back!

Dennis Lee

Hugger mugger

I'd sooner be
Jumped and thumped and dumped,

I'd sooner be
Slugged and mugged . . . than *hugged* . . .

And clobbered with a slobbering
Kiss by my Auntie Jean:

You know what I mean:

Whenever she comes to stay,
You know you're bound

To get one.
A quick
   short
   peck
   would
   be
   O.K.
But this is a
Whacking great
Smacking great
Wet one!

Kit Wright

When

When I'm an aunt I shan't
Sip tea and criticise,
Won't buy my nieces socks,
Or my nephews ties.
For birthdays I'll send monkeys,
White mice and pirate suits;
At Christmas sets for chemistry,
And tambourines and flutes.
At Easter I'll bring chocolate eggs,
Not hymn books of white leather,
And I'll never scold at muddy feet
Or dogs in rainy weather.
When I'm an aunt I'll never mind
Rough ball games on my lawn,
And even turn an eye that's blind
To pillow fights at dawn.

Shelagh McGee

Toffee's Chewy

Toffee's chewy

Toffee's chewy,
Treacle's gooey,
Ice cream's licky,
Honey's sticky,
Nuts are crunchy,
Chocolate's munchy . . .

All these things
I love to eat
But POPCORN is
My favourite treat.

Barbara Ireson

Spaghetti

Spaghetti, spaghetti, all over the place,
Up to my elbows – up to my face,
Over the carpet and under the chairs,
Into the hammock and wound round the stairs,
Filling the bathtub and covering the desk,
Making the sofa a mad mushy mess.

The party is ruined, I'm terribly worried,
The guests have all left (unless they're all buried).
I told them, 'Bring presents.' I said, 'Throw confetti.'
I guess they heard wrong
'Cause they all threw spaghetti!

Shel Silverstein

The greedy giant

There once was a giant
So far from compliant,
    He wouldn't eat toast with his tea.
'A substance so horrid
Brings pains in my forehead,
    And aches in my toe–toes,' said he, said he,
    'And aches in my toe–toes,' said he.

They brought him a tartlet
To cheer up his heartlet,
    They brought him both jelly and jam;
But still while he gobbled,
He sighed and he sobbled,
    'You *don't* know how hungry I am, I am,
    You don't *know* how hungry I am!'

They brought him a cruller
To make him feel fuller,
    They brought him some pancakes beside,
They brought him a muffin,
On which he was stuffin',
    When all of a sudden he died, he died,
    When all of a sudden he died.

Laura E. Richards

Yellow butter

Yellow butter purple jelly red jam black bread

Spread it thick
Say it quick

Yellow butter purple jelly red jam black bread

Spread it thicker
Say it quicker

Yellow butter purple jelly red jam black bread

Now repeat it
While you eat it

Yellow butter purple jelly red jam black bread

Don't talk
With your mouth full!

Mary Ann Hoberman

The Mouse, the Frog, and the Little Red Hen

Once a Mouse, a Frog, and a Little Red Hen,
    Together kept a house;
The Frog was the laziest of frogs,
    And lazier still was the Mouse.

The work all fell on the Little Red Hen,
    Who had to get the wood,
And build the fires, and scrub, and cook,
    And sometimes hunt the food.

One day, as she went scratching round,
    She found a bag of rye;
Said she, 'Now who will make some bread?'
    Said the lazy Mouse, 'Not I.'

'Nor I,' croaked the Frog as he drowsed in the shade,
    Ren Hen made no reply,
But flew around with bowl and spoon,
    And mixed and stirred the rye.

'Who'll make the fire to bake the bread?'
    Said the Mouse again, 'Not I,'
And scarcely opening his sleepy eyes,
    Frog made the same reply.

The Little Red Hen said never a word,
    But a roaring fire she made;
And while the bread was baking brown,
    'Who'll set the table?' she said.

'Not I,' said the sleepy Frog with a yawn;
    'Nor I,' said the Mouse again.
So the table she set and the bread put on,
    'Who'll eat this bread?' said the Hen.

'I will!' cried the Frog. 'And I!' squeaked the Mouse,
    As near the table they drew;
'Oh no, you won't!' said the Little Red Hen.
    And away with the loaf she flew.

Anon

Chips

Out of the paper bag
Comes the hot breath of the chips
And I shall blow on them
To stop them burning my lips.

Before I leave the counter
The woman shakes
Raindrops of vinegar on them
And salty snowflakes.

Outside the frosty pavements
Are slippery as a slide
But the chips and I
are warm inside.

Stanley Cook

Rhinoceros stew

Rhinoceros stew
Tastes like glue,
While giraffe casserole
Sticks to the bowl.
An emu roast
Tastes like burnt toast,
While pelican fried
Turns the inside.
But none of this feed
Encourages greed.

Michael Dugan

Spaceman's complaint

It's very difficult for me,
When I'm in space, to eat my tea.
I float about, I have no weight
And keep on going past my plate.

Barbara Ireson

The sea-serpent

A sea-serpent saw a big tanker,
Bit a hole in her side and then sank her,
    It swallowed the crew
    In a minute or two,
And then picked its teeth with the anchor.

Anon

Sneaky Bill

I'm Sneaky Bill, I'm terrible mean and vicious,
I steal all the cashews from the mixed-nuts dishes;
I eat all the icing but I won't touch the cake,
And what you won't give me, I'll go ahead and take.
I gobble up the cherries from everyone's drinks,
And if there's sausages I grab a dozen links;
I take both drumsticks if there's turkey or chicken,
And the biggest strawberries are what I'm pickin';
I make sure I get the finest chop on the plate,
And I'll eat the portions of anyone who's late!

I'm always on the spot before the dinner bell –
I guess I'm pretty awful,
                          but
                              I
                                 do
                                    eat
                                        well!

William Cole

When Betty eats spaghett

When Betty eats spaghetti,
She slurps, she slurps, she slurps.
And when she's finished slurping,
She burps, she burps, she burps.

Colin We

Jelly Jake and Butter Bill

Jelly Jake and Butter Bill
One dark night when all was still
Pattered down the long, dark stair,
And no one saw the guilty pair;
Pushed aside the pantry-door
And there found everything galore –
Honey, raisins, orange-peel,
Cold chicken aplenty for a meal,
Gingerbread enough to fill
Two such boys as Jake and Bill.
Well, they ate and ate and ate,
Gobbled at an awful rate
Till I'm sure they soon weighed more
Than double what they did before.
And then, it's awful, still it's true,
The floor gave way and they went through.
Filled so full they couldn't fight,
Slowly they sank out of sight.
Father, Mother, Cousin Ann,
Cook and nurse and furnace man
Fished in forty-dozen ways
After them, for twenty days;
But not a soul has chanced to get
A glimpse or glimmer of them yet.
And I'm afraid we never will –
Poor Jelly Jake and Butter Bill.

Leroy F. Jackson

The lion

The lion just adores to eat
A lot of red and tender meat,
And if you ask the lion what
Is much the tenderest of the lot,
He will not say a roast of lamb
Or curried beef or devilled ham

Or crispy pork or corned–beef hash
Or sausages or mutton mash.
Then could it be a big plump hen?
He answers 'No'. What is it, then?
Oh, lion dear, could I not make
You happy with a lovely steak?

Could I entice you from your lair
With rabbit pie or roasted hare?
The lion smiled and shook his head.
He came up very close and said,
'The meat I am about to chew
Is neither steak nor chops. It's you.'

Roald Dahl

The sausage

The sausage is a cunning bir
With feathers long and wavy
It swims about the frying pa
And makes its nest in gravy.

Ano.

Old Joe Clarke

Old Joe Clarke, he had a house,
Was fifteen storeys high,
And every darn room in that house
Was full of chicken pie.

I went down to Old Joe Clarke's
And found him eating supper;
I stubbed my toe on the table leg
And stuck my nose in the butter.

I went down to Old Joe Clarke's
But Old Joe wasn't in;
I sat right down on the red–hot stove
And got right up again.

Old Joe Clarke had a candy box
To keep his sweetheart in;
He'd take her out and kiss her twice
And put her back again.

Anon

A man of the dunes

A delicious old man of the dunes
dined sweetly on beach plums and prunes,
and danced by the ocean
in lovely slow motion
while humming the yummiest tunes.

N. M. Bodecker

The boy stood in the supper-room

The boy stood in the supper-room
   Whence all but he had fled;
He'd eaten seven pots of jam
   And he was gorged with bread.

'Oh, one more crust before I bust!'
   He cried in accents wild;
He licked the plates, he sucked the spoons –
   He was a vulgar child.

There came a burst of thunder-sound –
   The boy – oh! where was he?
Ask of the maid who mopped him up,
   The bread crumbs and the tea!

Anon

I scream

Nicodemus Nicholas Belvedere Brown
is the very best ice cream eater in town.
A cone or a cup,
he'll guzzle it up;
a sundae with sprinkles
gives him the twinkles.
Strawberry, banana, vanilla macaroon,
he can eat ice cream from here to the moon.
He dreams of chocolate chip, dish after dish,
and pistachio's his favourite flavourful wish.
He can't get enough
of the meltaway lipadrip lap-and-lick stuff.
Rocky road marshmallow! Orange mandarin!
Ginger peachy! Pack it all in!

'No,' says his mother, 'just one portion.'
'Well, then,' says Nick, 'may I pick the dish?'
'I guess,' says his mother, 'I guess you may.'
Says Nick, 'Hooray.'
'Then the dish that I pick is rather small,
Just the size of a red bouncing ball
that expands to be as big as a bed,
a bed that's so high and so wide and so deep
that inside it ten fat men can sleep
and a horse and a sheep can fit into it too,
along with a dolphin and a kangaroo,
and ten tall ships and ten more again,
and a forest and a farm and a factory and a mill,
and an airplane hangar and the highest hill. . . .'

'Stop!' says his mother.
'As soon,' says Nicky, 'as I fill the dish.'
'And that will be all?' his mother says,
'just that one dish that is round as a ball?'
'Of course,' says Nick, 'for I don't want a portion
that's too big, I wouldn't like to be a pig.'

Eve Merriam

Giants' delight

Vats of soup
On table trays
Side of shark
With mayonnaise
Haunch of ox
With piles of mice
Mounds of gristle
Served on ice
Bone of mammoth
Head of boar
Whales and serpents
By the score
Tons of cole slaw
Stacks of rabbits
(Giants have such
Piggy habits)
Then, at last,
There comes a stew
Full of buffalo
And ewe
Followed by
Some chocolate cakes
Big enough
For stomachaches

Steven Kroll

I wish I was a little grub
With whiskers round my tummy
I'd climb into a honey pot
And make my tummy gummy.

Anon

The ghostly grocer of Grumble Grove

in Grumble Grove, near Howling Hop
there stands a nonexistent shop
within which sits, beside his stove
the ghostly grocer of Grumble Grove.

there on rows of spectral shelves
chickens serenade themselves,
sauces sing to salted butter,
onions weep and melons mutter,

cornflakes flutter, float on air
with loaves of bread that are not there.
thin spaghettis softly scream
and curdle quarts of quiet cream,

phantom figs and lettuce spectres
dance with cans of fragrant nectars,
sardines saunter down their aisle,
tomatoes march in single file,

a cauliflower poltergeist
juggles apples, thinly sliced,
a sausage skips on ghostly legs
as raisins romp with hard-boiled eggs.

as pea pods play with prickly pears,
the ghostly grocer sits and stares
and watches all within his trove,
that ghostly grocer of Grumble Grove.

Jack Prelutsky

Minnie

Minnie can't make her mind up,
Minnie can't make up her mind!
    They ask her at tea,
    'Well, what shall it be?'
    And Minnie says, 'Oh,
    Muffins, please! no,
    Sandwiches – yes,
    Please, egg-and-cress –
    I mean a jam one,
    Or is there a ham one,
Or is there another kind?
    Never mind!
        Cake
    Is what I will take,
The sort with the citron rind,
    Or p'r'aps the iced one –
    Or is there a spiced one,
Or is there the currant kind?'
    When tea is done
    She hasn't begun,
She's always the one behind,
Because she can't make her mind up,
Minnie *can't* make up her mind!

Eleanor Farjeon

Snickles and Podes

Mean song

Snickles and podes,
Ribble and grodes:
That's what I wish you.

A nox in the groot,
A root in the stoot
And a gock in the forbeshaw, too.

Keep out of sight
For fear that I might
Glom you a gravely snave.

Don't show your face
Around any place
Or you'll get one flack snack in the bave.

Eve Merriam

Tea party

Mister Beedle Baddlebug,
Don't bandle up in your beedlebag
Or numble in your jimblejug,
Now eat your nummy tiffletag
Or I will never invite you
To tea again with me. Shoo!

Harry Behn

Piffing

Effily Offily
If If If
Niffily Noffily
Piff Piff Piff
I've Piffed at the Baker
I've Piffed at the Beak
Effily Offily
Squeak Squeak Squeak

Spike Milligan

Hitting

Use a log to hit a hog.
Use a twig to hit a pig.
Use a rake to hit a snake.
Use a swatter to hit an otter.
Use a ski to hit a bee.
And use a feather when you hit me.

Shel Silverstein

It was shut

'Sam, shut the shutter,' Mother Hyde
Called, her cap-strings all a-flutter.
'I've shut the shutter,' Sam replied;
'And I can't shut it any shutter.'

J. T. Greenleaf

Frying pan in the moving van

A new family's coming to live next door to me.
I looked in the moving van to see what I could see.
>
> *What did you see?*
> *Tell, tell, tell.*

Well,
I saw a frying pan in the moving van.
>
> *What else did you see?*
> *Tell, tell, tell.*

Well,
I saw a rocking chair and a stuffed teddy bear
and a frying pan in the moving van.
>
> *What else did you see?*
> *Tell, tell, tell.*

Well,
I saw a rug for the floor and a boat with an oar
and a rocking chair and a stuffed teddy bear
and a frying pan in the moving van.
>
> *What else did you see?*
> *Tell, tell, tell.*

Well, I saw a leather boot and a basket of fruit
and a rug for the floor and a boat with an oar
and a rocking chair and a stuffed teddy bear
and a frying pan in the moving van.
>
> *What else did you see?*
> *Tell, tell, tell.*

Well, I saw a TV set and a Ping-Pong net
and a leather boot and a basket of fruit
and a rug for the floor and a boat with an oar
and a rocking chair and a stuffed teddy bear
and a frying pan in the moving van.
>
> *What else did you see?*
> *Tell, tell, tell.*

Well, I saw a steamer trunk and a double-decker bunk
and a TV set and a Ping-Pong net
and a leather boot and a basket of fruit
and a rug for the floor and a boat with an oar
and a rocking chair and a stuffed teddy bear
and a frying pan in the moving van.
What else did you see?
Tell, tell, tell.

Well, I saw a lamp with a shade and a jug of lemonade
and a steamer trunk and a double-decker bunk
and a TV set and a Ping-Pong net
and a leather boot and a basket of fruit
and a rug for the floor and a boat with an oar
and a rocking chair and a stuffed teddy bear
and a frying pan in the moving van.
What else did you see?
Tell, tell, tell.

Well, since you ask it:
I saw a wicker basket
and a violin and a rolling pin and a vegetable bin
and a lamp with a shade and a jug of lemonade
　　and a garden spade
and a steamer trunk and a double-decker bunk
　　and a Chinese model junk
and a TV set and a Ping-Pong net
　　and a framed silhouette
and a leather boot and a basket of fruit
　　and a baseball suit
and a rug for the floor and a boat with an oar
　　and a knob for a door
and a rocking chair and a stuffed teddy bear
　　and plastic dinnerware
and an electric fan and a bent tin can
　　and a frying pan and
THAT'S ALL I SAW IN THE MOVING VAN.

Eve Merriam

Circles

The things to draw with compasses
Are suns and moons and circleses
And rows of humptydumpasses
Or anything in circuses
Like hippopotamusseses
And hoops and camels' humpasses
And wheels on clownses busseses
And fat old elephumpasses.

Harry Behr

The cow

The cow mainly moos as she chooses to moo
and she chooses to moo as she chooses.

She furthermore chews as she chooses to chew
and she chooses to chew as she muses.

If she chooses to moo she may moo to amuse
or may moo just to moo as she chooses.

If she chooses to chew she may moo as she chews
or may chew just to chew as she muses.

Jack Prelutsky

Pop bottles pop-bottles

Pop bottles pop-bottles
   In pop shops
The pop-bottles Pop bottles
   Poor pop drops

When Pop drops pop-bottles
   Pop-bottles plop!
Pop-bottle-tops topple
   Pop mops slop!

Anon

The sniffle

In spite of her sniffle,
Isabel's chiffle.
Some girls with a sniffle
Would be weepy and tiffle;
They would look awful,
Like a rained-on waffle,
But Isabel's chiffle
In spite of her sniffle.
Her nose is more red
With a cold in her head,
But then, to be sure,
Her eyes are bluer.
Some girls with a snuffle,
Their tempers are uffle,
But when Isabel's snivelly
She's snivelly civilly,
And when she is snuffly
She's perfectly luffly.

Ogden Nash

Busy day

Pop in
pop out
pop over the road
pop out for a walk
pop in for a talk
pop down to the shop
can't stop
got to pop

got to pop?

pop where?
pop what?

well
I've got to
pop round
pop up
pop in to town
pop out and see
pop in for tea
pop down to the shop
can't stop
got to pop

got to pop?

pop where?
pop what?

well
I've got to
pop in
pop out
pop over the road
pop out for a walk
pop in for a talk. . . .

Michael Rosen

Smiling villain

Forth from his den to steal he stole,
His bags of chink he chunk,
And many a wicked smile he smole,
And many a wink he wunk.

Anon

The dripping tap

Drip drap
Goes the dripping tap,
Drip drap.

Flit flot
Into the old jampot,
Flit flot!

Plashes plishes
Over the unwashed dishes,
Plashes plishes!

Dillery dullery
All over the scullery,
Dillery dullery!

Tink tonk tank
On the draining-board plank,
Tink tonk tank!

Bink bankety bunk
On a pile of junk,
Bink bankety bunk!

Junk in the sink?
That's a bit odd, I think,
Junk in the sink!

But so is the pink
Of a dripping tap in the kitchen sink,
Pink! Pink! Pink!

James Kirkup

Who'd be a Juggler?

Who'd be a juggler?

Last night, in front of thousands of people,
he placed a pencil on his nose
and balanced a chair upright on it
while he spun a dozen plates behind his back.
Then he slowly stood on his head to read a book
at the same time as he transferred the lot
to the big toe of his left foot.
They said it was impossible.

This morning, in our own kitchen,
I ask him to help with the washing-up –
so he gets up, knocks over a chair,
trips over the cat, swears, drops the tray
and smashes the whole blooming lot!
You wouldn't think it was possible.

Cicely Herbert

Timothy Grady

Poor little Timothy Grady
Screwed up his face at a lady,
And, jiminy jack!
It wouldn't come back.
The louder he hollered
The tighter it grew,
His eyes are all red
And his lips are all blue.
Oh, mercy me, what in the world will he d
Poor little Timothy Grady!

Leroy F. Jacks

Glasshouse Street

Don't throw stones in Glasshouse Street,
    In Glasshouse Street,
    In Glasshouse Street,
Don't throw stones in Glasshouse Street,
    Or you'll be – beat!

Two small boys in Glasshouse Street,
One March morning happened to meet –
    A stone flashed,
    A window smashed
    A chimney pot crashed,
    And the boys were thrashed!

So *don't* throw stones in Glasshouse Street,
    In Glasshouse Street,
    In Glasshouse Street,
Don't throw stones in Glasshouse Street,
    Whoever – you – meet!

Eleanor Farjeon

Clumsy Clarissa

Clarissa did the washing up:
She smashed a plate and chipped a cup,
And dropped a glass and cracked a mug,
Then pulled the handle off a jug.
She couldn't do much worse, you'd think,
But then she went and broke the sink.

Colin West

Polly Picklenose

'Polly, Polly, goodness gracious!
You just quit your making faces.'
Polly laughed at what they said,
Cocked her nose and went to bed.

But the big black Bugoo heard,
And he came without a word;
Walked right in – you bet a nickel!
In his hand a great green pickle;

Stalked along with steady pace,
Stuck it right in Polly's face,
Pinned it fast, and there it grows –
Poor Polly Picklenose!

Leroy F. Jackson

Accident

I took my girl to a ball one night
And sat her down to supper,
The table fell and she fell too,
And stuck her nose in the butter.

Scottish Children's Skipping Song

Tilda Tidbury

Tilda Tidbury
Went to school
With a nice clean face
And a cap of wool.
A skirt of yellow
And socks of blue.
A silver buckle
On each bright shoe.

Tilda Tidbury
Went to school
And saw a butterfly
Near a pool.
Its wings were silver
With dots of red;
It glittered and fluttered
Above her head.

Tilda Tidbury
Gave a jump
And down she came
With a great big thump!
Her shoes were muddy
And splashed her skirt;
Her little white cap
Was covered with dirt!

The silver butterfly
Flew right up,
Then lightly slid
To a buttercup.
There he turned to a queer little man,
Laughed ho! ho!
And off he ran.

L. H. Allen

Margaret Nash got wet but I don't know how

Margaret Nash
Went swimming – splash! –
Right in the middle of the Ocean.
'What? Swimming where?
Who took her there?'
– I haven't the slightest notion.

She jumped from a ship
And cut her lip
According to the Squid.
She fell from a plane
That was going to Spain
That's what Fish say she did.

She fell from a cloud
She wasn't allowed –
Except in dreams – to ride.
It changed to rain
And she couldn't remain.
Or so I'm told by the Tide.

She paddled on toast
Away from the coast
According to the Whale.
The toast soaked thin.
Margaret fell in.
– But what an unlikely tale!

What a pack of lies;
It's just not wise
To trust what you hear in the Ocean.
And truth to tell
The fact is – well,
I haven't the slightest notion.

John Ciardi

The wishing well

I climbed up on the wishing well
And looked right down.
Then in I fell!

The walls of the well
Are covered in slime.
They're much too slippery
For me to climb.

All I can do
Is holler and shout:
'I WISH that someone
Would get me out!'

Barbara Ireson

Help!

Catch hold of my leg!
Catch hold of my toe!
I'm flying away
And I don't want to go.

I bought this balloon
Just a minute ago
From the man with a beard
Who's still standing below.

Why didn't he tell me,
Why didn't he say
A balloon of this size
Would just fly me away?

Catch hold of my leg!
Catch hold of my toe!
I'm flying away
And I don't want to go.

Barbara Ireson

Hugh

There was a young fellow called Hugh
Who went to a neighbouring zoo.
   The lion opened wide
   And said, 'Come inside
And bring all your family too.'

Max Fatchen

Little Dimity

Poor little pigeon-toed Dimity Drew,
The more she ate, the smaller she grew.
When some people eat, they get taller and taller;
When Dimity ate, she got smaller and smaller.
She went for a walk, and all you could see
Was a tam-o'shanter the size of a pea,
An umbrella as big as the cross on a *t*,
And a wee pocketbook of butterfly blue.
She came to a crack one half an inch wide,
Tripped on a breadcrumb, fell inside,
And slowly disappeared from view.

William Jay Smith

Gobbling and squabbling

In a very old house
On a street full of cobbles,
Two very old ladies
Have got colly-wobbles,

And out on the pavement
The neighbours are grumbling,
And sighing, 'Oh *when* will
Their stomachs stop rumbling?'

Kit Wright

I used to have a little red alarm clock

I used to have a little red alarm clock.
It was my dad's.
He gave me it
and I used to keep it by the side of my bed.

It was very small and it had legs
only the legs were like little balls –
little metal balls,
and you could unscrew them
out of the bottom of that little red clock.

One morning
I was lying in bed
and I was fiddling with my clock
and I unscrewed one of those
little ball–leg things
and, do you know what I did?
I slipped it into my mouth – to suck
like a gob-stopper.

Well it was sitting there,
underneath my tongue
when I rolled over
and – ghulkh – I swallowed it:
the leg off my clock.
It had gone. It was inside me. A piece of metal.

I looked at the clock.
It was leaning over on its side.
I stood it up and of course it fell over.

So I got up,
went downstairs with it
and I was holding it out in front of me
and I walked in to the kitchen
and I said:
'Look, the clock. The leg. The leg. The clock – er . . .'

And my dad took it off me and he said,
'What's up, lad? Did you lose it?
Not to worry, it can't have gone far.
We'll find it,
and we can screw it back on here, look.'

'I swallowed it,' I said.

'You swallowed it? You swallowed it?
Are you mad? Are you stark staring mad?
You've ruined a perfectly good clock.
That was a good clock, that was. Idiot.
Now what's the use of a clock that won't stand up?'
He held it out in front of him,
and he stared at it. I looked at it too.
I was wondering what was happening to the leg.

Michael Rosen

Oh Erica, not again!

Every time we go on the pier,
   Or down to the sea, that is,
Erica says she is feeling queer
   And it makes her poor head whizz.

Erica says she likes the land,
   And there isn't, alas, much doubt,
As soon as she steps on a trippers' boat
   Erica's legs give out.

Erica's hands will clutch the rail.
   She hears the timbers creak.
She wonders where the lifebelts are –
   Or if we've sprung a leak.

There's never a sign of storm or gale
   But mother's crying 'Quick!'
And so it's just the same old tale,
   Erica's sick!

Max Fatchen

The fox rhyme

Aunt was on the garden seat
   Enjoying a wee nap and
Along came a fox! teeth
   Closed with a snap and
He's running to the woods with he
   A–dangle and a–flap and –
Run, uncle, run
   And see what has happened!

Ian Serraillie

This is a stick-up!

The world seems full of sticky,
It's everywhere I go,
Underneath the table,
And it's moving to and fro.

It follows me to school each day,
It gets into my books,
I swear that I don't put it there
But that's the way it looks.

I've got sticky on my fingers,
Sticky on my clothes,
Sticky inside my pockets,
Sticky up my nose.

My mother keeps on scrubbing
To wash the stick away,
The flannel just gets stuck to me,
My stick is here to stay!

She's hidden all the treacle
And all the sweets she can,
She's locked up all the Syrup
And every pot of Jam.

So *why* am I so sticky
And nicknamed Sticky Sam?
I really-*really* can't believe
How stuck up I am.

Spike Milligan

Time machine

If ever you should want to go
Into the future, let me know.
My new machine can carry you
Forward to 1992.

You'd really like to try today?
No time like now, I always say.
We'll get inside and shut the door,
I'll show you what the knobs are for.

Now please don't touch the one that's red.
Just use the blue and green instead.
The green one first and then the blue,
You'll soon see what you have to do.

You must have heard me when I said
That you must NEVER touch the red.
Oh dear! Oh dear! Look what you've done –
We're back in 1621.

Barbara Ireson

Adolphus Elfinstone

Adolphus Elfinstone of Nachez
Thought it fun to play with matches
Until the little Goop had learned
It hurt a lot when he got burned!
A *little* fire is queer and curious;
But soon it grows quite big and furious.

Gelett Burgess

Take Your Paws Off Me!

Take your paws off me!

Take your paws off me.
I really don't see
Why a tiger like you,
That lives at the zoo,
Should have my bun.
It's my only one,
Take your paws off me.

Barbara Ireson

The reason for the pelican

The reason for the pelican
Is difficult to see:
His beak is clearly larger
Than there's any need to be.

It's not to bail a boat with –
He doesn't own a boat.
Yet everywhere he takes himself
He has that beak to tote.

It's not to keep his wife in –
His wife has got one, too.
It's not a scoop for eating soup.
It's not an extra shoe.

It isn't quite for anything.
And yet you realise
It's really quite a splendid beak
In quite a splendid size.

John Ciardi

A house is a house for me

A hill is a house for an ant, an ant,
A hive is a house for a bee.
A hole is a house for a mole or a mouse
And a house is a house for me!

A web is a house for a spider,
A bird builds its house in a tree.
There is nothing so snug as a bug in a rug
And a house is a house for me!

Mosquitoes like mudholes or puddles.
Whales need an ocean or sea.
A fish or a snake may make do with a lake
But a house is a house for me.

A glove is a house for a hand, a hand.
A stocking's a house for a knee.
A shoe or a boot is a house for a foot
And a house is a house for me.

And once you get started in thinking this way
It seems that whatever you see
Is either a house or it lives in a house,
And a house is a house for me.

A flower's at home in a garden,
A donkey's at home in a stall.
Each creature that's known has a house of its own
And the earth is a house for us all.

Mary Ann Hoberman

Geraldine Giraffe

The
longest
ever
woolly
scarf
was
worn
by
Geraldine
Giraffe.
Around
her
neck
the
scarf
she
wound,
but
still
it
trailed
upon
the
ground.

Colin West

Odd

That's
odd
I must
say.

As I sat
on the
stump,
a piece of road
took
a lively
jump.

A small brown
clod
leaped
up
and away.

A piece of road!

Well, it *might*
have been
a tiny
toad.

Lilian Moore

The giraffe and the woman

Sing a song of laughter
    About the young giraffter
Who tried to reach the rafter
    To get the apple-pie;
The woman put it there, you know,
'Cause she was in despair, you know,
'He reaches everywhere, you know,
    And eats until I cry!'

Sing a song of laughter!
    The greedy young giraffter,
He got what he was after,
    And it was piping hot!
It burnt his mouth so terribly,
He yelped and yammered yerribly,
The woman chuckled merrily,
    And said, 'See what you got!'

Laura E. Richards

Hedgehog

He ambles along like a walking pin cushion,
Stops and curls up like a chestnut burr.
He's not worried because he's so little.
Nobody is going to slap him around.

Chu Chen Po
(translated by Kenneth Rexroth)

Two octopuses

Two octopuses got married
And walked down the aisle
Arm in arm in arm
Arm in arm in arm
Arm in arm in arm
Arm in arm in arm

Remy Charlip

Allie, call the birds in

Allie, call the birds in,
The birds from the sky.
Allie calls, Allie sings,
Down they all fly.
First there came
Two white doves,
Then a sparrow from his nest,
Then a clucking bantam hen,
Then a robin red–breast.

Allie, call the beasts in,
The beasts, every one.
Allie calls, Allie sings,
In they all run.
First there came
Two black lambs,
Then a grunting Berkshire sow,
Then a dog without a tail,
Then a red and white cow.

Allie, call the fish up,
The fish, from the stream.
Allie calls, Allie sings,
Up they all swim.
First there came
Two gold fish,
A minnow and a miller's thumb,
Then a pair of loving trout
Then the twisted eels come.

Allie, call the children,
Children from the green.
Allie calls, Allie sings,
Soon they run in.
First there came
Tom and Madge,
Kate and I, who'll not forget
How we played by the water's edge
Till the April sun set.

Robert Graves

Message from
a caterpillar

Don't shake this
bough.
Don't try
to wake me
now.

In this cocoon
I've work to
do.
Inside this silk
I'm changing
things.

I'm worm–like now
but in this
dark
I'm growing
wings.

Lilian Moore

A big Brontosaurus

A big Brontosaurus lay counting
As he breathed from the top of his head –
He started at one,
And when he was done,
'I'm two hundred years old!' he said.

Barbara Ireson

So big!

The dinosaur, an ancient beast,
I'm told, was very large.
His eyes were big as billiard balls,
His stomach, a garage.
He had a huge and humping back,
A neck as long as Friday.
I'm glad he lived so long ago
And didn't live in my day!

Max Fatchen

The frog and the toad

Hopping frog, hop here and be seen,
I'll not pelt you with stick or stone:
Your cap is laced and your coat is green;
Good–bye, we'll let each other alone.

Plodding toad, plod here and be looked at,
You the finger of scorn is crooked at:
But though you're lumpish, you're harmless too;
You won't hurt me, and I won't hurt you.

Christina Rossetti

Hippos

Though hippos weigh at least a tonne,
They love to wade and wallow,
They never sink.
I sometimes think
A hippo must be hollow!

Doug Macleod

Hippopotamuses

Hippopotamuses never
Put on boots in rainy weather.
To slosh in mud up to their ears
Brings them great joy and merry tears.
Their pleasure lies in being messed up
They just won't play at being dressed up.
In fact a swamp is heaven plus
If you're a hippopotamus.

Arnold Spilka

At the zoo

First I saw the white bear, then I saw the black;
Then I saw the camel with a hump upon its back;
Then I saw the grey wolf, with mutton in his maw;
Then I saw the wombat waddle on the straw;
Then I saw the elephant a-waving of his trunk;
Then I saw the monkeys – mercy, how unpleasantly they
smelt

William Makepeace Thackeray

The house mouse

Little brown house mouse, laugh and leap,
chitter and cheep while the cat's asleep,
chatter and call and slip through the wall,
trip through the kitchen, skip through the hall.

Little brown house mouse, don't be meek,
dance and squeak and prance and tweak.
There's cheese to take and plenty of cake
as long as you're gone when the cat's awake.

Jack Prelutsky

Mice

I think mice
Are rather nice.

Their tails are long,
Their faces small,
They haven't any
Chins at all.
Their ears are pink,
Their teeth are white,
They run about
The house at night.
They nibble things
They shouldn't touch,
And no one seems
To like them much.

But I think mice
Are nice.

Rose Fyleman

Glowworm

Never talk down to a glowworm –
Such as *What do you knowworm?*
How's it down belowworm?
Guess you're quite a slowworm.
No.   Just say
                    Hellowworm!

David McCord

Full of the moon

It's full of the moon
The dogs dance out
Through brush and bush and bramble.
They howl and yowl
And growl and prowl.
They amble, ramble, scramble.
They rush through brush.
They push through bush.
They yip and yap and hurr.
They lark around and bark around
With prickles in their fur.
They two–step in the meadow.
They polka on the lawn.
Tonight's the night
The dogs dance out
And chase their tails till dawn.

Karla Kuskin

The walrus

The widdly, waddly walrus
has flippery, floppery feet.
He dives in the ocean for dinner
and stands on his noggin to eat.

The wrinkly, crinkly walrus
swims with a debonair splash.
His elegant tusks are of ivory
and he wears a fine walrus moustache.

The thundery, blundery walrus
has a rubbery, blubbery hide.
He puffs up his neck when it's bedtime
and floats fast asleep on the tide.

Jack Prelutsky

Who's in?

'The door is shut fast
And everyone's out:'
But people don't know
What they're talking about!
Say the fly on the wall,
And the flame on the coals
And the dog on his rug,
And the mice in their holes,
And the kitten curled up,
And the spiders that spin –
'What, everyone's out?
Why, everyone's in.'

Elizabeth Fleming

The giggling gaggling gaggle of geese

The giggling gaggling gaggle of geese,
they keep all the cows and the chickens awake,
they giggle all night giving nobody peace.
The giggling gaggling gaggle of geese.

The giggling gaggling gaggle of geese,
they chased all the ducks and the swans from the lake.
Oh when will the pranks and the noise ever cease
of the giggling gaggling gaggle of geese!

The giggling gaggling gaggle of geese,
it seems there's no end to the mischief they make,
now they have stolen the sheep's woollen fleece.
The giggling gaggling gaggle of geese.

The giggling gaggling gaggle of geese,
they ate all the cake that the farmer's wife baked.
The mischievous geese are now smug and obese.
The giggling gaggling gaggle of geese.

The giggling gaggling gaggle of geese,
eating that cake was a dreadful mistake.
For when holiday comes they will make a fine feast.
The giggling gaggling gaggle of geese.

Jack Prelutsky

Worm

Worm
Is a term for a worm.
It sounds like a worm looks
Slow
Low to the ground
Usually brown
It would never have feathers
It would not sing at all
With a name like worm
It must be long and thin
And crawl.

Karla Kuskin

Worm

Little worm – wiggle wiggle,
You make me and my sister giggle.
You live in mud,
You live in wet,
You never ever see a vet,
You must be very healthy worm,
Wiggle Wiggle Wiggle Squirm.

Spike Milligan

The dog on the beach

As we sit on the beach,
Just preparing to eat,
A dog comes snuffing from group to group,
Shuddering a share of salt drops on each,
And flapping his damp tail;
He noses my spade and pail;
But when I reach to pat him –
(Brown eyes that beg,
And sea–wet coat all matted with sand) –
He makes one dart, and snatches the
Sandwich out of my hand!

John Walsh

A bumble-bee

What do I see?
A bumble-bee
Sit on a rose
And wink at me!

What do you mean
By 'hum, hum, hum'?
If you mean me,
I dare not come!

Anon

Index of titles

Index of first lines

ndex of authors

155

Acknowledgements

The authors and publishers would like to thank the following people for giving permission to include in this anthology material which is their copyright. The publishers have made every effort to trace copyright holders. If we have inadvertently omitted to acknowledge anyone we should be grateful if this could be brought to our attention for correction at the first opportunity.

Joan Allen for 'Tilda Tilbury' from *Round about Eight* by L. H. Allen.

Atheneum Publishers for 'It isn't', 'I scream', and 'Frying pan in the moving van' from *A Word or Two with You* by Eve Merriam; for 'Mean song' from *There is No Rhyme for Silver* by Eve Merriam; for 'Snowy morning', 'The Troll Bridge', and 'The red kite', from *Something New Begins* by Lilian Moore; and for 'Message from a caterpillar', 'Odd', 'I wish', 'Lost and found', 'The witch's garden', 'I never saw', 'Bedtime story', and 'The witch's song', from *See my Lovely Poison Ivy* by Lilian Moore.

Avon Books, The Hearst Corporation for 'Did you?' from *A Boy Named Mary Jane and Other Silly Verse* by William Cole.

Mrs Joyce Burnell for 'Kangaroo shoe' by Dorothy Barnham.

Jonathan Cape Limited for 'The lion' by Roald Dahl.

Carousel Books, Transworld Publishers Ltd for 'Windscreen wipers' from *A Bright Red Lorry*, 'Under my bed' and 'A big brontosaurus' from *Oh Dinosaur!*, and 'Spaceman's complaint' and 'Time machine' from *Spaceman, Spacemen*, all © Copyright by Barbara Ireson.

Miss D. E. Collins and A. P. Watt & Son Ltd for 'Triolet' from *The Coloured Lands* by G. K. Chesterton.

Stanley Cook for 'Chips' from *Come Along: Poems for Younger Children* by Stanley Cook, published by the author, 600 Barnsley Road, Sheffield S5 6UA.

Curtis Brown Ltd for 'Hullabaloo' by Ursula Moray Williams, © Copyright Ursula Moray Williams 1969. Reprinted by permission of Curtis Brown Ltd, London on behalf of Ursula Moray Williams.

Curtis Brown Ltd, New York for 'The Sniffle' from *Verses From 1929 On* by Ogden Nash, © Copyright 1941 by The Curtis Publishing Company; and for 'Hickenthrift and Hickenloop' and 'Whose boo is whose' from *The Phantom Ice-cream Man* by X. J. Kennedy.

M. Dent & Sons Ltd for 'A man of the dunes' from *A Person from Britain* by N. M. Bodecker.

André Deutsch Ltd for 'Every few weeks someone looks at me. . . .' from *You Can't Catch Me!* by Michael Rosen; and 'I've had this shirt' from *Mind Your Own Business* by Michael Rosen.

Dodd, Mead and Co Inc for 'Advice to children' by Carolyn Wells from *Baubles*.

Faber and Faber Ltd for 'Lazy Lucy' and 'Mr 'Gator' from *Let's Marry Said the Cherry* by N. M. Bodecker.

Norma Farnes for 'Granny' from *Silly Verse for Kids* by Spike Milligan; for 'The Wiggley-Woggley Men' from *The Bedside Milligan* by Spike Milligan; for 'Kangaroo-Kangaroo!', 'Granny's boot', and 'This is a stick-up!' from *Unspun Socks* by Spike Milligan; and for 'Multikertwigo', 'Worm', and 'Piffing' by Spike Milligan.

Elizabeth Fleming for 'Who's in?' by Elizabeth Fleming.

Robert Graves for 'Allie, call the birds in' by Robert Graves.

Greenwillow Books for 'The walrus', 'The cow', 'The house mouse', and 'The giggling, gaggling gaggle of geese' by Jack Prelutsky from *Zoo Doings*.

Harcourt, Brace Jovanovich, Inc for 'Tea party' from *Windy Morning* and 'Circles' and 'Hallowe'en' from *The Little Hill*, all by Harry Behn.

Harper & Row Inc for 'The sitter', 'Always sprinkle pepper in your hair' and 'Bear in there' from *A Light in the Attic* by Shel Silverstein; for 'Snowman' and 'Spaghetti' from *Where the Sidewalk Ends* by Shel Silverstein; for 'Do you know the man' by Shel Silverstein from *Oh, How Silly!*; and for 'Hitting' by Shel Silverstein; for 'Okay, everybody, listen to this' from *Near the Window Tree* by Karla Kuskin; for 'Full of the moon' and 'Tiptoe' from *In the Middle of the Trees* by Karla Kuskin; for 'The witches ride' from *The Rose on my Cake* by Karla Kuskin; and for 'Worm' by Karla Kuskin; for 'Engineers' by Jimmy Garthwaite from *Puddin' an' Pie*; for 'I like it when it's mizzly' from *I Like Weather* by Aileen Fisher; for 'What night would it be?' from *You Read to Me, I'll Read to You* by John Ciardi; for 'Oh, such silliness' by William Cole from *Oh, such Foolishness*; and for 'Sneaky Bill' by William Cole from *Oh, That's Ridiculous!* by William Cole.

George Harrap Ltd and Little, Brown and Company for 'Every time I climb a tree' from *Every Time I Climb a Tree* by David McCord, © Copyright 1952 by David McCord.

Cicely Herbert for 'Who'd be a juggler' by Cicely Herbert.

David Higham Associates Ltd for 'A kitten' from *Silver Sand and Snow* by Eleanor Farjeon; 'Minnie', 'Glasshouse Street' and 'Cottage' by Eleanor Farjeon; and 'Quack! said the Billy-Goat' from *Figgie Hobbin* by Charles Causley, published by Macmillan London.

Holiday House Inc for 'Singing Ghost' by Stephen Kroll; and for 'Giant's delight' by Steven Kroll and 'Shrieks at midnight' by Dorothy Brown, both from *Giant Poems*.

Holt, Rinehart & Winston Inc for 'The dark gray clouds' by Natalia M. Belting from *The Sun is a Golden Earring*.

Houghton Mifflin Company Inc for 'Questions! Questions! Questions!' and 'Suzie's new dog' by John Ciardi from *Fast and Slow*.

Hutchinson Publishing Group for 'My obnoxious brother Bobby', 'Cousin Jane', 'The Ogglewop', 'When Betty eats spaghetti', 'Clumsy Clarissa', 'Geraldine Giraffe', 'Jocelyn, my dragon', 'Sir Hector' from *Not to be Taken Seriously* by Colin West, 'Names' by Norman Hunter and 'Fingummy' by Mike Harding from *Never Wear Your Wellies in the House* (ed. Tom Baker), published by Sparrow Books.

Ruth W. Jackson for 'Jelly Jake and Butter Bill', 'Polly Picklenose' and 'Timothy Grady' from *The Peter Patter Book* by Leroy F. Jackson, published by Rand McNally and for 'Grandpa dropped his glasses' by Leroy F. Jackson, from *Child Life Magazine*. Used by permission of his heir Ruth W. Jackson.

James Kirkup for 'Cosy catnap' and 'The dripping tap' by James Kirkup.

J. B. Lippincott Inc for 'Summer song' by John Ciardi; for 'Margaret Nash got wet but I don't know how' by John Ciardi from *The Man who Sang the Sillies*; and for 'The reason for the pelican' from *The Reason for the Pelican* by John Ciardi.

The Literary Trustees of Walter de la Mare and The Society of Authors as their representative for 'Grim' by Walter de la Mare.

Little, Brown & Company for 'The greedy giant' and 'The giraffe and the woman' from *Tirra Lirra* by Laura E. Richards; and for 'Glowworm' from *Every Time I Climb a Tree* by David McCord, © Copyright 1962 by David McCord.

Russell & Volkening Inc and Alfred A. Knopf Inc for 'Yellow butter' from *The Looking Book* by Mary Ann Hoberman.

James McGibbon, executor of the Estate of Stevie Smith, for 'Fairy Story' from *The Collected Poems of Stevie Smith* (Allen Lane).

McIntosh & Otis Inc for 'A giant named Stanley' by Michael Patrick Hearn.

Macmillan Publishing Inc New York for 'The ghostly grocer of Grumble Grove' and 'Huffer and Cuffer' from *The Ghostly Grocer of Grumble Grove* by Jack Prelutsky; and for 'Don't ever seize a weasel by the tail' from *A Gopher in the Garden* by Jack Prelutsky.

Macmillan of Canada for 'I found a silver dollar' and 'Billy Batter' from *Alligator Pie* by Dennis Lee.

Methuen London Ltd for 'I'll Buy a Peacock Bird' by Modwena Sedgwick from *All Sorts 7*; and for 'Missing' from *When We Were Very Young* by A. A. Milne.

Oxford University Press for 'Mrs Golightly' from *Blackbird in the Lilac* by James Reeves (1952). Reprinted by permission of Oxford University Press.

Penguin Books Ltd for 'My Granny is a witch' by Arkady Mikhailov from *Russia's Other Poets*, edited by Bosley; for 'Be quiet', 'Fred', 'Oh Erica, not again!', 'My dog', 'So big' and 'Catnap' from *Songs for my Dog and Other People* by Max Fatchen, published by Kestrel Books; and 'Who's scared now', 'Hugh' and 'Hair' by Max Fatchen; for 'Babbling and gabbling' by Kit Wright from *Hot Dog and Other Poems*, published by Puffin Books; and for 'Busy day' and 'I used to have a little red alarm clock' from *You Tell Me* by Michael Rosen, published by Kestrel Books.

Punch Publications Ltd for 'Noise' by J. Pope.

Joan Langford Reed for 'The Britons of old' by Langford Reed.

Robson Books for 'Frogday' and 'Shopping list' from *Witches* by Shelagh McGee and for 'When' from *Smile Please* by Shelagh McGee.

Scholastic Inc for 'Teeny tiny ghost' by Lilian Moore, reprinted from *Spooky Rhymes and Riddles* by Lilian Moore, ©Copyright 1972 by Lilian Moore. Reprinted by permission of Scholastic Inc.

Ian Serraillier for 'The Fox Rhyme' ©Copyright 1950 Ian Serraillier.

The Society of Authors as the literary representative of the Estate of Rose Fyleman for 'Mice' by Rose Fyleman.

Nancy Willard and Rita Scott, Inc for 'The games of night' from *Ghost Poems* by Nancy Willard.

New Directions Publishing Corporation for 'Hedgehog' by Chu Chen Po, translated by Kenneth Rexroth, from *One Hundred More Poems from the Chinese,* ©Copyright 1970 by Kenneth Rexroth. Reprinted by permission of New Directions Publishing Corporation.

The Viking Press Inc for 'A house is a house for me' by Mary Ann Hoberman.

Mrs A. M. Walsh for 'Goldfish' and 'The dog on the beach' by John Walsh.

MARY HAD A CROCODILE AND OTHER FUNNY ANIMAL VERSE

Jennifer Curry

Inside these pages you'll meet all kinds of animals. There's a slinking lynx and rats with felt hats. You'll discover why the crocodile had toothache and what happened when a giant gorilla came to tea. And just in case you should chance upon a Horny-Goloch or Cyril the Centipede, you'll know exactly what to say . . .